21 Dirty Tricks in Negotiation

The book for negotiators who want to work with awareness and integrity.

Mike Phipps - Politics at Work

Frances Tipper – SpokenWord Ltd

The Legal Stuff

Copyright © Mike Phipps and Frances Tipper 2016

The authors hereby assert their right to be identified as the authors of this work in accordance with sections 77 to 78 of the Copyright, Designs and Patents Act 1988.

All rights reserved. No part of this book may be reproduced in any form or by any electronic or mechanical means, including information storage or retrieval systems, without permission in writing from the publisher, except by a reviewer who may quote brief passages.

ISBN: 978-1539816799

Contents

1. The Lock In Game — 10
2. The Fool's Gold Game — 15
3. Divide and Conquer Game — 19
4. Cherry Picking Game — 23
5. Bluffing Game — 27
6. The Good Cop Bad Cop Game — 31
7. The Brinkmanship Game — 35
8. Time Bandit Game — 39
9. Stonewalling Game — 43
10. Emotional Outburst Game — 47
11. Scrambled Eggs Game — 52
12. The Hole in my Pocket Game — 56
13. All Change Game — 60
14. The Better Offer Game — 65
15. Reluctant Player Game — 69
16. No Authority — 73
17. Intimidation Game — 78
18. Russian Front Game — 82
19. Split the Difference Game — 87
20. The Walk Away Game — 91
21. The Withdrawn Offer Game — 96
22. The Nibble Game — 101

Acknowledgments

We would like to thank the kind, meticulous and painstaking work of Stephanie Tipper, Edward and Di Bartley for their editing and proofing expertise.

The front cover, spine and back were designed by the extremely creative Guy Farrow at Victory Art.

And the most patient, wonderfully knowledgeable and helpful Rebecca Emin who turned our work into a book.

Our sincere thanks to these two experts.

We would also like to thank our dedicated colleagues Andrew Hatcher and Saul Cambridge for their unfailing enthusiasm in running the chaos of the Dark Arts negotiation carousel with us, mostly successfully.

Finally, our gratitude to Anna Helga Tandberg Solheim for allowing us to run the Defence of the Dark Arts negotiation carousel for the first time during the Developing International Negotiators training programme at Statoil. It is now a regular and extremely valuable feature of all our negotiation courses.

A quick word, before you dive in.

We have spent years training and coaching experienced negotiators and they all ask exactly the same question. What do we do when we face a counterparty that uses dirty tricks? They can sense something is going wrong in the negotiation and they end up walking away with a bad deal, and sometimes they can't even work out why.

For a long time, we tried to avoid including anything about dirty tricks in our training programmes, because our focus was on best behaviours and getting the all-important "win-win". To be seen training people in what we termed the "Dark Arts" of negotiation was, we considered, not particularly ethical.

But in our own negotiations around the world, we knew that these dirty tricks are not used by a few unscrupulous companies. Not at all. These tactics are openly discussed and employed by top international companies, in trade disputes and most definitely between governments as part of their negotiation strategies.

So, like all the other books in the 21 Dirty Tricks series, awareness of what is really going on and learning how to counter games effectively is essential. And so our "Defence Against the Dark Arts" training in negotiation was born, with a grateful nod to Harry Potter.

We would never suggest you use any of these tactics, but we do strongly recommend you learn about them before you go into any negotiation. You may feel you have a really good relationship with your counterparty, and indeed, they may be lovely people, who visit their mums regularly and are kind to kittens, but business negotiations are competitive and can be cruel. Your counterparty is not there to look after you. They are there to get the best deal for themselves, not you - although they really do like you - a lot! So they say.

The bad news is that these games can and do get played, simply because they work. But in order to work, they rely on your ignorance. This book will save you from being exploited at the negotiation table.

21 Dirty Tricks in Negotiation brings together some of the worst and most used tactics encountered in international negotiations. We describe the tactic, and importantly, how you feel when you're being pushed into making the wrong move in the negotiation. We show you how to recognise when you're being played by a ruthless counterparty and, best of all, we show you exactly how you can uncover the game and take control of the negotiation.

Let's get practical for a moment.

For each of the negotiation games in this book there is a short description followed by a concise commentary, so each game is clear in your thinking and you will be able to recognise it.

We then draw a distinction between when this is a legitimate negotiation tactic and where it tips over into being a game.

More importantly though, we also provide strategy ideas for how to resolve the game and some powerful questions you can ask your counterparty. These questions need to be adapted to your specific, real situation.

And asking these types of questions is vital. Questions help us to get information and uncover what is really going on, so if we want to confront a game, questions help us find safer, more certain ground.

Questions keep the negotiation alive and give us more thinking time and, importantly, if it is indeed a game being played, it increases pressure on those who would manipulate us. This can be important because when we invite them into a more honest dialogue, it gives them an easier way out. Helping a counterparty save face can be vital if you are negotiating a long-term arrangement where the quality of the relationship is important.

Finally, for each game, there is a short section called Antidote in Action (see the next page). This is a simple 4-step process that increases your chances of success. The first two sections are always the same, but the final two steps are customised for each tactic being explored. There is more about this on the next page.

Antidote in Action

For every negotiation game analysed, the first two stages are always the same. This simple but powerful 4-step process is not a silver bullet solution, but it increases your chances of being successful.

Take It

This is about taking responsibility for your own thinking, feeling and behaviour. Keep calm, remain diplomatic and use your emotional intelligence.

Explore It

Use the top 10 example questions provided for each tactic to help unpick what is really going on and invite the other party into a more productive dialogue.

The last two stages have variations specific to each of the games and require a little more attention and creativity.

(Name It)

This is always described in brackets. It is an optional step, because demonstrating your awareness that your counterparty is playing a game is often the hardest to do and might damage the relationship. So you won't always want to take that action. That is okay, because the final stage below is often the most potent.

Change It

Finding new ways to move the negotiation on so that a "win-win" outcome can be achieved, the relationship can be protected and our counterparty can save face. Searching for new, creative options to discuss changes the direction of the game and opens up new and better possibilities.

What is your negotiation style?

Free "thank you" offer.

Our Negotiation Style Questionnaire (NSQ) supports all our Negotiation Skills Workshops. It delivers instant report describing your natural style with all of your inherent strengths, as well as the development areas you might need to address to become the best negotiator you can be.

And as a thank you for buying this book, you get to try it out for free. Simply email our partners at info@stylequestionnare.com letting us know your name, surname, job title and organisation and we will send you the on line invite.

Please treat this offer ethically. Only one application per book purchase, please.

1. The Lock In Game

You are presented with a list of preconditions that rule out important aspects of the negotiation and limit your options before you even start.

You have won the internal influencing campaign inside your business. You have passed through all the decision gates, aligned your stakeholders and now have a realistic mandate from your senior management. Everyone is onside, you have a team all briefed and ready to go for the first round of face-to-face negotiations. You want to cautiously celebrate because you know that often the internal negotiation is harder than the external. And you did it!

You email across to your counterparty a suggested agenda for the first round of negotiations, but you get back a list of preconditions that not only take you by surprise, but it is a list that you can never agree to. Preconditions are not so unusual in negotiations, but these items would lock you into a bad position before you start, will limit your power and take important deal drivers off the table.

You had not expected the first round of negotiations to be via email, but that is what happens. They won't budge on the preconditions and you can't accept them. It is deadlock, and you haven't even started! As it stands a "win-win" deal is not possible. It could be that the preconditions are valid concerns that your counterparty has, but their determined anchoring over them ahead of face-to-face negotiations might also be the start of the Lock In Game.

NOT a negotiation trick:

If or when the preconditions are industry standard, or can be justified as legitimate concerns that counterparties sometimes have e.g. health and safety, or security.

Probably a negotiation trick:

If or when they stubbornly anchor, won't provide a justified rationale and it will alter the dynamics in their favour.

What to do:

In the event of the Lock In Game, a safe place to start is to suggest that you meet face to face as soon as possible, not to begin, but to negotiate how the negotiations are to be negotiated. Yes, really. We are used to pre-meetings and meetings about meetings, so this is not so different. Yes, it's time consuming, not especially efficient, and not how you want to start, but you need to break the deadlock. This approach gives you the advantage of starting to build the relationship and to investigate their concerns (valid or otherwise) behind the preconditions. If they won't agree to this, then it increases the certainty that this is a Lock In Game.

A second option is to consider escalating to your senior management, and suggest they do the same. This is awkward because you don't want to appear lacking in ability to conduct the negotiations, but in the event of deadlock, getting an initial agreement over preconditions at a more senior level can be helpful.

A third option is to suggest that a sub-team meet to work on the preconditions in parallel with the real negotiations. These might be from legal, compliance or procurement, people who speak the same language and who will know the industry standard agreements. This means that you show respect for their preconditions, but have the possibility of progress on other, more important matters.

The Lock In Game

In the unlikely event that you have been using email as the only communication channel, then pick up the phone and call your counterparty. Ensure you are mentally prepared and have good questions and some creative options ready. If you make the call you will be prepared and there is a strong possibility that they will be less so. A call also demonstrates your willingness to get started, as well as your confidence to initiate the difficult conversation. You position yourself as the problem solver rather than the blocker.

Walking away is always an option. If they rule out all possibility of a "win-win" deal before you start, then why go ahead? Having tried all the above, having to walk away "with regret" tests the importance and even the validity of their preconditions. If the deal is as important to them as you think it might be, suggesting that you are walking away tests their resolve and means they have to make the next move.

And remember, they will have to go back to their management and declare a no deal before the start. Not a great position for them, given that they probably had to influence those same management to give them a mandate in the first place.

Top Questions to Ask:

- Help me to understand these preconditions.
- What is the importance of each of these precondition items to you?
- Can you tell me how you think this helps the negotiation process?
- Can we meet and create a set of mutually agreeable preconditions?
- How else would you suggest we make progress?
- How about if my boss calls your boss to see if that helps?
- How about we put our legal people together to work on these preconditions?

The Lock In Game

- Before we leave the table, can we summarise where we are so far in the negotiation? (Repeated at the end of every meeting.)

The Lock In Game

Antidote in Action

Take It:

Keep calm and use your emotional intelligence.

Explore It:

Use the top questions above.

(Name It:)

Find a non-punishing way to surface what is really going on (if you feel that the risk is worth it).

"Your preconditions are limiting our ability to even get to the table. I cannot understand your insistence on this."

Change It:

Propose new, creative options for negotiation.

"I would like to propose that we look at other options that would satisfy us both so that we can start to make progress."

2. The Fool's Gold Game

They keep making apparently unimportant things seem essential, and then they concede them. Why?

You respect this counterparty team as being tough, determined negotiators, but you are struggling to understand what their interests really are. They say that the most important issue on the list for them is a "must have". They argue it's not a cost issue, it's more logistical but you really don't understand why that is so essential for them. Worse still, their "must have" is extremely difficult for you to give up and stay in mandate. But they are adamant, keen to do the deal and, hey, it's a negotiation, so you work out how you can compromise on other issues.

They signal that if you could only move on this issue, then there is a deal on the table. Because they offer you this glimmer of hope, you offer options and concessions in other areas. And as soon as you have compromised to meet their wish list, they drop everything that was apparently so important before. In fact their original "must have" now doesn't seem to have been a big issue at all. Is that because you found other solutions for them and you were wise to compromise? You step back and begin to reflect on how little they moved during the negotiation, and you realise with a sinking feeling that you've been lured into a bad deal.

The deceptive glitter of the Fool's Gold game is well known and often used as a negotiation strategy. It is so common that it is almost a standard trading strategy. The counterparty identifies an issue that is of little value to them, but of extreme importance to you. They hold on to this particular issue, pushing you until you make more and more concessions in other areas. But they don't concede on anything. You fall into this trap because you lose sight of the bigger picture. You are persuaded, mistakenly, that you're getting a good deal. Your counterparty gets the gold, not you, and you've been tricked by the Fool's Gold game.

NOT a negotiation trick:

When the counterparty can back up their arguments clearly on why the issue is important to them and they are willing to compromise in areas that are important to you.

Probably a negotiation trick:

If or when the item you negotiated so hard over suddenly becomes disposable or unimportant, it creates confusion or wears you and your team down. You begin chasing after Fool's Gold and give away too much without getting back anything of value.

What to do:

The Fool's Gold game is a deception that can make even experienced negotiators think they have a really good deal. Don't rush to make a deal just because they are offering it to you on a golden platter. Remember, if something sounds too good to be true, then it probably isn't.

Go back to negotiation basics. Ask your counterparty about their interests and priorities, and then probe and explore each one of these more deeply. Use "What if" scenarios to see how essential each item is to them. That way you're testing the validity of their arguments, rather than letting them push you into compromising on a single issue. If something really is important to them, it will be consistent not transactional.

When it comes to your offer, put two options on the table which allows them to compare all the variables –

the first puts them at a financial disadvantage but you've moved slightly on their most important issue, the second puts them in a better position. From their next move you immediately get a sense of what their real priorities are. They may well decide to drop the Fool's Gold Game early in the process when they realise the tactic is not working.

Both sides have to investigate creative options and consider alternatives. Both sides have to move. For every small concession they demand, ask them for options and what they can offer you. Remember always to trade, not just give stuff away. It's a negotiation, not a fire sale.

Top Questions to Ask:

- Can you explain what you want from the deal and why?
- Can you tell us your reasons why this is your top priority?
- What positive (or negative) impact does this issue have on the deal for your company (or bottom line)?
- By how much do the pros outweigh the cons?
- How do you reach your figures?
- If this is so important to you, what can you offer us in return?
- What are your suggestions and alternatives to help us resolve this issue?
- What's next on your list and why?
- What can you do to help us move on this?
- Before we leave the table, can we summarise where we are so far in the negotiation? (Repeated at the end of every meeting.)

The Fool's Gold Game

Antidote in Action

Take It:

Keep calm and use your emotional intelligence.

Explore It:

Use the top questions above.

(Name It:)

Find a non-punishing way to surface what is really going on (if you feel that the risk is worth it).

"You say this is your top priority and yet your arguments and numbers don't seem to support that. If it is that essential to you, what can you do to help us move on this?"

Change It:

Propose new, creative options for negotiation.

"Rather than get stuck on this issue, let's take a time out to look at a different scenario that works by putting this to one side."

3. Divide and Conquer Game

Your counterparty recognises that your deal team is not aligned and works to widen the split and weaken your power.

Your legal and technical experts are both new to your negotiation team. You spent some time going through the deal issues before the first meeting and feel confident about their background and expertise. You're sure they will perform well in the negotiation. When technical issues are raised during the meeting, you gladly look to your expert to answer the question and put forward your arguments. To your horror, you hear *your* expert not only agree with theirs but also strengthen *their* argument. You do your best to hide your shock and interrupt quickly to put across your side's position, only to see your expert shaking his head and making it very apparent that he disagrees with you.

They disguise it well, but you can see a glint of triumph from your counterparty and they instantly begin discussing the issue with your technical expert, not you. You are being pushed out and you're losing the argument on *both* sides of the table.

You are furious. What is going on? Is this stupidity, carelessness or incredibly unprofessional behaviour from a member of your team? You sit there, fuming, knowing you are going to have to ride this out, but you'll have more than just "a word" with them at the end of the meeting. Your instinct is to remove them immediately but would that be wise? They are a liability, damaging your credibility, your position and your strength in the negotiation. Your counterparty is making the most of it and revelling in the Divide and Conquer Game.

Divide and Conquer Game

NOT a negotiation trick:

Any counterparty will appreciate agreement from your side and will see this as a positive development in the negotiation. When they use it to move the negotiation forward rather than look to discredit or undermine you, they are not manipulating the situation as part of a trick.

Probably a negotiation trick:

When your counterparty turns it to their advantage, deliberately cultivates the misalignment and uses it to break your arguments and get what they want.

What to do:

Prevention is better than the cure. Create a strong negotiation team to prevent your counterparty from stripping you of your power by using the Divide and Conquer Game. For them, it is a joy to look across the table and face an unaligned negotiation team. Make sure everyone on your team knows their role and the roles of others. Each member should listen carefully to each other and support arguments seamlessly. The team must be disciplined and all the members must be completely aligned on the strategy. You can see instantly when a team has individuals working towards their own goals rather than a single, team goal.

Make sure you have an agreed plan and objective for every meeting and clear communication signals within the team when any member of the team feels the need for a time out to realign the strategy.

The counterparty will always be on the alert for misalignment. Some even employ behavioural analysts to sit on their team and watch for non-verbal clues that signal possible disagreements on the other side. Should they start to divide the team, signal for an immediate time out so you can make sure your team is realigned.

If the focus moves away from you to an unaligned team member, politely question the judgement of your counterparty. Such a petty move is counterproductive. It undermines the trust between the teams and so makes the deal harder to negotiate.

Your counterparty can only be effective in using the Divide and Conquer Game if you have an ineffective team lead or misaligned team. Make sure you don't give them the opportunity to use it.

Top Questions to Ask:

- Can we summarise the meeting so far and then take a short break?
- You appear to be asking the same question again and again. What exactly is unclear?
- Again, can you direct your questions on this to me?
- Can you clarify your point on this issue?
- You are causing great confusion with this. Can I reiterate our position?
- Can we write up on the board the outstanding issues for discussion?
- I believe we have covered this issue extensively. Can we summarise and move on to the next item on the agenda?
- We're not getting anywhere in this meeting. Can we take a time out and both sides return with their key priorities?
- Before we leave the table, can we summarise where we are so far in the negotiation? (Repeated at the end of every meeting.)

Divide and Conquer Game

Antidote in Action

Take It:

Keep calm, be assertive and take control.

Explore It:

Use the top questions above.

(Name It:)

Find a non-adversarial way to call the tactics and change the behaviours and dynamics in the room. Refocus the negotiation on the problem at hand.

"We are wasting a great deal of time on this issue and these discussions are not productive. Let's summarise and move on."

Change It:

Propose new dynamics and focus for the negotiation.

"We are not getting anywhere in this meeting. Let's take a break and both sides return to explain their interests and position on this issue."

4. Cherry Picking Game

Your counterparty gathers as many bids as possible before coming to push you into making an even better offer

You have presented your proposal to your counterparty and they have spent the entire meeting challenging you, systematically, on every line item. For every issue, they tell you that your pricing is too high compared to your competitors. They claim that your competitors are offering them much better prices, so you will need to at least match them if you want to do the deal.

You would expect that from a well-prepared counterparty. They are doing a very thorough job comparing offers from your competitors and you respect that they want to get the best price. However, you know your competitors and have a good sense of your market and its pricing. You know that some have better rates in certain areas and you have heard of others using temporary discounts. Yet the prices quoted to your counterparty from your competitors, on every single line item, are *all* better than yours. You know you are going to have to work hard to beat them.

You look for areas to trade with your counterparty, but they are not interested in giving anything back in return. They just want you to beat the competitor's price. You ask them for details of the competitor but they won't reveal who quoted this incredible offer. They hide behind commercial sensitivity. You start to feel suspicious. Individually, these numbers are possible, but as a package, unlikely, given your experience. You feel you're being forced to give in but you don't want to lose this deal. Is your counterparty really being offered a "dream deal" from somewhere else? Or, have they selected the best individual prices from a range of your competitors, so as to create the most profitable package for themselves by using the Cherry Picking Game?

NOT a negotiation trick:

When the counterparty is willing to share their competitive information with you and you recognise there is a major change in market pricing, then it is not a trick and the market information is useful for you to know.

Probably a negotiation trick:

When your counterparty quotes individual prices from across a range of competitors to create an artificial deal that tricks you into lowering your prices unnecessarily.

What to do:

Before getting to any negotiation table, your preparation will always include checking your market for the latest intelligence, trends and standards. So, when you feel that the "dream deal" a counterparty asks for sounds too good to be true, you may well be right, especially if it does not match your own market research. Your counterparty may have met with each of your competitors and then "cherry picked" the best prices from each of your competition's proposals.

Be direct. Ask them who in your market place could afford to offer them such a deal that is outside the industry norms? For them to share that information will build trust, but to withhold it will generate suspicion. And they will know this. If your counterparty is still reluctant to reveal the name of your competitor, it strengthens the possibility that they have been cherry picking. It is important to remember that your counterparty is still here, negotiating with you. Why are they still here if their "dream deal" is elsewhere?

Yes, a competitor may have offered a better price on one item, but you know that they have a different pricing structure in other areas where you are more competitive. Challenge your counterparty and propose that they look at the whole package rather than individual price items.

Point out that you are looking to negotiate a deal where both parties trade and discuss mutual concessions. Explain that in order to make the deal worthwhile you need to gain something in return for varying your offer. Help them out by suggesting options that benefit you such as a longer contract, greater quantity, or better terms. Be clear that they need to evaluate the agreement as a whole and they can't push you to do the "dream deal" as it simply doesn't exist.

Top Questions to Ask:

- Who offered you this dream deal?
- Did this dream deal come in one proposal?
- Why are you still here when your dream deal is elsewhere?
- What can you give us in return if you want us to offer a similar dream deal?
- What are the key issues that you want us to focus on?
- We agree that the price you quoted on that issue is low. Who offered you this?
- Can you explain the context of this particular quote?
- Rather than looking at individual items, can we focus on the deal as a whole?
- How does that one item meet your overall objectives for this deal?
- Before we leave the table, can we summarise where we are so far in the negotiation? (Repeated at the end of every meeting)

Cherry Picking Game

Antidote in Action

Take It:

Keep calm, be assertive and take control.

Explore It:

Use the top questions above.

(Name It:)

Find a non-adversarial way to call the tactics and change the behaviours. Refocus the negotiation on the problem at hand.

"Each of these prices are possible to find in the market, but only when they are quoted individually from across a range of providers, so we need to look at the package as a whole. Agreed?"

Change It:

Propose new dynamics and focus for the negotiation.

"Looking at individual items is not practical in this market. Let us start to look for mutual concessions that will create a deal that works for both of us."

5. Bluffing Game

They give you incorrect information, hide essential facts, or exaggerate their position to give themselves an advantage in the negotiation.

Your counterparty has just put a set of numbers on the table and their initial explanation appears to be valid. As you delve deeper into the numbers, you begin to feel uncomfortable and suspicious. You want to trust what they say but the assumptions upon which their numbers are based just don't make sense. Indeed the more you explore, the more dubious they seem. Your instinct tells you that something is not quite right and as you continue to question, they resort to not answering and then they deliver a doomsday scenario. They say that they have to stick with their numbers in order to keep the plant running and their operators employed. Do you push them to reduce their numbers and risk the plant closing, or is something deceptive going on?

In a well-planned, professional negotiation, both sides will have an information- sharing strategy. It is a plan for what information to disclose and when to disclose it. The sharing of information is what moves every negotiation forward and should build trust in the relationship. But is that information accurate and honest? Your counterparty might not tell the whole truth if they believe that to do so would undermine their position. They might decide to bluff. Bluffs are deliberately deceptive moves to create the impression of a stronger position, or to give the illusion of confidence about an uncertain issue in order to influence or deter. You need to know how you can you differentiate between a bluff and the truth. And it often starts in the gut. When you feel uneasy about their information and you get a sense that there is no real substance behind your counterparty's brash confidence, you could be on the receiving end of the Bluffing Game.

NOT a negotiation trick:

When your counterparty answers your questions directly and openly, when they are willing to share information with you and, together with your own research, you are satisfied that you have reliable and trustworthy information.

Probably a negotiation trick:

When your counterparty avoids answering your questions directly, is inconsistent in their replies, sounds overconfident without substance and is reluctant to look you in the eye. When something doesn't quite feel right, be open to the fact that your counterparty may be using the Bluffing Game.

What to do:

Whenever you get that nagging feeling that your counterparty is either hiding something or not telling you the complete truth, you need to ask probing questions and be persistent with your questioning. Do not be fobbed off with vague or unsubstantiated replies. Ask for evidence to back up numbers, look for corroboration of the details, check the rationale and justification of their arguments and get verification and proof wherever possible.

If your counterparty appears uncomfortable with any of your questions, be tenacious; keep asking until you are satisfied with the answers. Notice the body language. Is it congruent with the words they are saying? Some people can sound positive, but their body language tells a different story, perhaps displaying nervous movements or gestures and too little eye contact. And what do you make of those slightly shifty interactions between your counterparty's team members?

Bluffing Game

Be persistent, check and double check their answers until you know you have uncovered all their bluffs. And then you will have a decision to make. Do you want to press the advantage and punish them for their deception? Or, do you want to offer them a way to save face, protect the relationship and move forwards in the deal, safe in the knowledge that you now have the right information?

Top Questions to Ask:

- What exactly did you mean by that? Can you give me more detail?
- What is your justification for that?
- What are the underlying calculations behind that amount?
- Is there anything you have missed out?
- Sorry, I didn't quite understand. Can you help by giving me an example?
- Can you show us the numbers so we understand how you reached that decision?
- Can you clarify the figures, as these don't seem to make sense to us?
- Can you explain your reasons for making such a statement?
- What evidence do you have to verify these figures?
- Based on your numbers, how can you demonstrate the validity of your argument?
- Before we leave the table, can we summarise where we are so far in the negotiation? (Repeated at the end of every meeting.)

Bluffing Game

Antidote in Action

Take It:

Keep calm, be assertive and take control.

Explore It:

Use the top questions above.

(Name It:)

Find a non-adversarial way to call the tactics and change the behaviours and dynamics in the room. There is no need to endure bad behaviour in a meeting. Call it for what it is. Refocus the negotiation on the problem at hand.

"There seems to be some inconsistencies here. Can you explain your assumptions and give us the rationale behind these numbers?"

Or

"You say you have access to these resources which is great news for you. What evidence can you show us to verify and support this information?"

Change It:

Propose new dynamics and focus for the negotiation.

"You say that your only option is to close the plant. Can we look at all aspects of the deal and really drill into the numbers to see what other options are open to us?"

6. The Good Cop Bad Cop Game

The good cop wants to help you get the deal done before the bad guy comes back and ruins everything.

The negotiation has been getting more and more intense. One person on the counterparty team seems especially frustrated and they are getting increasingly angry. They bang the table, shout and point at you. They make accusations and use language that would make a construction worker blush. They throw their papers up in the air and stride about the room, and with arms flailing, they wail at how unfair and unreasonable you are being. You marvel at how that vein throbbing on their forehead does not burst. Finally, they get up, they deliver a final threat and they storm out of the room. There is a tumbleweed moment of eerie silence.

Another member of the counterparty's team turns to you and offers an immediate apology. They say that their colleague is under tremendous pressure and that they are easily provoked. They say we are not to worry, the deal is still on, but they also suggest we need to make rapid progress while the Bad Cop is out of the room. They tell us that a key concession now would calm the situation down and be good for the relationship. If not, they can't guarantee what might happen next.

Negotiators have contrasting styles. Some are reasonable and others less so. That's life. But when two very contrasting styles play off each other as described above, we need to be aware of the Good Cop Bad Cop Game.

Not a Negotiation Game:

If the bad cop is from one of the more emotionally expressive cultures, or when one negotiator has modelled their style and approach on the tough guys they have seen in movies and genuinely thinks that will be effective.

The Good Cop Bad Cop Game

Probably a Negotiation Game:

When there is a foil in the room who balances the bad guy and, one on one, is just so kind to you that you suddenly feel seduced into wanting to help them.

What to do:

You can of course simply match their unreasonable behaviour with your own unreasonable behaviour. Indeed, sometimes turning up the heat in a negotiation can move the process on, but this comes at significant risk. The relationship might suffer a terminal shock. And can you really go back to your boss with the news that you behaved unreasonably, but still didn't get the deal? Or, that you did get the deal, but the relationship is now so bad that the five-year contract is going to be hell for everyone.

Neither can you allow yourself to be seduced into concessions with the good cop. Explaining to your boss that you gave your mandate away because the good cop was Mr Nice Guy is just as bad, both for your business and your career.

Emotional intelligence is key. Both the good and bad cop behaviours are tactics to coerce you into conceding something that under normal circumstances you would not do. But somewhere, underneath all that tactical posturing there are two negotiators who badly want something, but are not expressing it authentically. And you are going to help them with that, because that is good business.

The key is to keep a tight control over your own emotions. It is important to regard unreasonable behaviour only as an *invitation* to feel threatened or intimidated, not an *instruction*. And similarly, you must not be seduced by kindness.

You might want to take a time out, you might feel you need it; however, the strongest position to take is to show that none of the tactical behaviours are having any impact on you. Stay calm, go back to the agenda and signal your intent to keep working. In a steady voice, ask similar questions to the suggestions below. Under these conditions you have demonstrated your professionalism, whereas they have lost the moral high ground by behaving like children. Relax, you now have an advantage.

Top Questions to ask:

- What agenda item shall we focus on while we wait?
- Where do you think there might be an opportunity for us to get quick mutual agreement?
- What was your colleague's intent by behaving like that?
- What do they really want?
- Would you like a few moments to go and get your colleague back? I want to press on.
- How can I help you get this deal done despite your colleague's behaviour?
- While they are out of the room, it is now safer for you to raise any issues that might be more difficult for you with them here. What's on your mind?
- If all this behaviour is about getting concessions, can you tell me what is important to you so that we can start getting creative?
- Before we leave the table, can we summarise where we are so far in the negotiation? (Repeated at the end of every meeting.)

The Good Cop Bad Cop Game

Antidote in Action

Take It:

Keep calm and use your emotional intelligence.

Explore It:

Use the top questions above.

(Name It:)

Find a non-punishing way to surface what is really going on (if you feel that the risk is worth it).

"Your colleague really isn't helping this negotiation much. Why don't we take this opportunity to find a better way forward?"

Change It:

Propose new, creative options for negotiation.

"Tell your colleague we are continuing and we would value them returning just as soon as they are ready."

7. The Brinkmanship Game

Your counterparty pushes you to the "brink" of catastrophe in order to get the best terms for themselves.

The unions are unhappy. You have already spent three days discussing their outrageous demands. They are threatening a strike to force you to agree to their requirements. You know that a strike would damage your business badly and it would attract very negative publicity. To give in at this stage of the deal would appear weak and would encourage them to ask for yet more next time.

You are furious with them. They are pushing you to accept a deal which is completely unfair. The terms are extortionate. You tell them they are making a mistake. Their members will lose wages if they go on strike, so it will hurt them just as much as you. Their demands are so unreasonable that, if you agreed, you would have to reduce the workforce to pay for them. So both sides lose if they go on strike and both sides lose if you give in to their demands.

The deadline looms. You're being pushed to the very edge and the pressure is intense. You feel you have no way out. It seems you're going to lose whatever you do. Weighing up your potential losses, minutes before the deadline, you back down reluctantly. Did you have a choice? That nagging question you keep asking yourself is still unanswered. Who gains the most from this deal? It certainly wasn't fair. You have a suspicion that the unions have a better deal. If they have gained more than you from this deal through intimidation, they may well have been using the dangerous, damaging and extreme Brinkmanship Game.

NOT a negotiation trick:

When both parties stand to lose the same amount and there is no unfair advantage for either side.

Probably a negotiation trick:

When the counterparty aggressively pushes for an unfair deal to the point where you are forced to either give in, or stop the negotiations.

What to do:

Brinksmanship is a kind of bullying. It is explicitly unfair as a tactic, so your natural response is likely to be emotional. You will probably be angry and will want to push back as hard as you can, even when you know that your counterparty is dragging you over the precipice with them.

First you need to have an accurate and objective assessment of exactly what each party has to gain or lose. Second, you need to show your counterparty that you know exactly what they have to gain or lose. This reduces the strength of their threat, and by becoming factual the emotional intensity is reduced. You will have a slight advantage too if your counterparty doesn't have all the information about your potential gains and losses, so do your best to maintain that edge.

Above all, you have to convince them that you are absolutely dedicated to your position, while leaving the possibility of compromise open. Be as sweetly *un*reasonable as possible in an open and logical fashion. Make sure you appear cooperative and friendly in order to minimise any emotional responses.

These three elements undermine their Brinkmanship Game. They discourage the hostile posturing of your counterparty, send a clear signal that you're not going to give in and also allow the possibility of building a bridge that will let your counterparty pull back.

Top Questions to Ask:

- How much do you consider you will lose by not doing a deal?
- What are your underlying costs of a no deal?
- What are the consequences for you if there is no deal?
- What are your potential gains if we reach a deal?
- What are the positive and negative impacts for you, deal or no deal?
- We're both fixed in our positions so can we both take some time to consider creative options that would add value for both of us?
- Can we agree that the deadline is a goal and use the time now to break down this issue into more logical pieces?
- The costs are significant on both sides so can we consider how best to minimise them in the long term?
- We both look to lose extensively if we fail to reach an agreement. Can we assess how we both can gain in real value terms from a deal?
- Before we leave the table, can we summarise where we are so far in the negotiation? (Repeated at the end of every meeting.)

Antidote in Action

Take It:

Keep calm and use your emotional intelligence.

Explore It:

Use the top questions above.

(Name It:)

Find a non-punishing way to surface what is really going on (if you feel that the risk is worth it).

"Can you explain why you are prepared to go down this damaging route which hurts both of us, without first exploring all the possibilities?"

Change It:

Propose new, creative options for negotiation.

"We're both stuck in our positions, so can we both go away and come back with suggestions and ideas to add some value to the deal?"

8. Time Bandit Game

They impose a deadline, limiting the time available and insist that it is now or never.

Having spent months negotiating with a number of missed end dates, you reluctantly agree to a firm deadline to complete the deal. You now have a few hours to go and you feel the pressure of that deadline becoming more intense. Your counterparty keeps reminding you of the deadline and now they say that they have arranged a press conference for the agreed time. You are reluctant to request a new deadline in case it would make you appear weak and you don't want to be the one who is blamed for failing to reach an agreement. Your counterparty pushes again, if you can't close the deal now, time runs out and the deal is off the table. You have come too far to throw all that work away. But you don't have time to discuss the minor concessions your counterparty demands. They seem acceptable, but there is no time to run the numbers. You feel intense pressure to just agree to everything, sign and hope for the best.

But beware. The Time Bandit Game is about unfairly, or dishonestly, using time lines in the negotiation. And it can take all kinds of guises from the one above where you have agreed to a formal deadline, to false, needless deadlines imposed on you by a ruthless counterparty. Another variation is for long drawn out delays where the counterparty misses every deadline, and the "fatigue and discomfort" variation, where the counterparty insists that you work late into the night, to exhaust you into submission.

When under time pressure, it is easy to lose sight of the overall objective and you can give in too easily and make fundamental mistakes. You might feel forced to make a last minute deal when you have had no time to discuss the consequences with your team, assess whether the deal fits within your strategy, or even more critically, within your mandate. You cannot allow time to be used tactically against you and you need to control it, or risk being caught out by the Time Bandit Game.

NOT a negotiation trick:

When you have jointly agreed the deadline at the beginning of the negotiation, together with the process, and timetable for meeting that deadline. And, if either side need to change that, then it is discussed and a new time line agreed.

Probably a negotiation trick:

When your counterparty imposes a deadline and insists that the deadline cannot change. When they use the deadline to force you to make a deal, your counterparty is using the Time Bandit Game to pressure you into making mistakes or concessions.

What to do:

One of the most essential rules in negotiation is to make sure you are always in control of time and to never let others control you with time. When you are pushed for time in any negotiation, you are more likely to make mistakes and rush to decisions that you will regret.

Remain calm, put aside the deadline and stick to your original strategy. Insist on having time to discuss everything with your team and, yes, run the numbers. Find out how much every concession will cost you and then make sure you get the equivalent back. It's a two way street – do not let them push you to give anything away for free.

Time Bandit Game

So they've organised a press conference in 5 minutes? The press can wait. Your requirement to get the right deal for you is far more important. They want to carry on through the night? Be assertive, state your desire to complete the deal and carry on the negotiation after a break. They refuse to commit to a deadline? Agree to a process instead. Always set goals rather than deadlines so that the Time Bandit can't steal the deal from you.

Top Questions to Ask:

- Why is this deadline so important to you?
- What are the consequences of moving the deadline?
- Can we discuss and agree on the process and how we manage the timetable going forwards?
- We need a timeout to discuss these last minute requests. Do you have any other issues that we need to take away with us?
- Can you explain why you have introduced several new items at the last minute?
- If these items are so essential to you, why have you not raised them before now when we are minutes away from completing the deal?
- Are these really that essential that you want to postpone closing the deal?
- Can we agree to come back with top priorities and then suggest a new timetable and process to follow?
- If you're worried about committing to a deadline, can we agree a process and general timeline so we can keep the negotiation moving?
- Before we leave the table, can we summarise where we are so far in the negotiation? (Repeated at the end of every meeting.)

Time Bandit Game

Antidote in Action

Take It:

Keep calm, be assertive and take control.

Explore It:

Use the top questions above.

(Name It:)

Find a non-adversarial way to call the tactics and control the time element.

"I agree that we can try to aim for your deadline. Let's keep this as a goal and see how we manage with the time we have."

Change It:

Propose new dynamics and focus for the negotiation.

"You say now or never, so can you help us to understand why this deadline is so important to you? Then we can find the best way of working with you on this."

9. Stonewalling Game

Your counterparty deliberately gives vague responses and makes any form of communication extremely difficult.

The negotiation started well. You appeared to be building a good relationship and discussing the issues openly in each meeting, but not any more. Now you find every meeting excruciating, progress is almost non-existent. It is like wading through treacle.

Your counterparty seems to be avoiding any serious commitment on the key issues. They waste a great deal of time by having long time outs with their team. When you ask questions to find out what's happening, they give vague answers and mostly ignore the question, or don't respond at all. It is increasingly hard to hold any kind of conversation and you may as well be talking to a brick wall.

You have no idea why they are dragging their feet. You are extremely frustrated as you're not getting any results, and your management want an update. So what can you do? You decide to put another offer on the table with a few new concessions to see if that will reignite the negotiation process, or have you just been tricked by the Stonewalling Game?

NOT a negotiation trick:

It is not a negotiation trick if your counterparty is able and willing to give you their reasons for suddenly cooperating less.

Stonewalling Game

Probably a negotiation trick:

Where no reasons are offered for their refusal to cooperate and they want to trick you into impulsive or careless concessions.

What to do:

Not every refusal to cooperate or slow down the process is stonewalling. There may be a justifiable reason why your counterparty has suddenly hit the negotiation brakes and stopped cooperating. This is unusual, but it can happen.

A shrewd stonewaller will probably have conceded on some of the lesser issues and even moved from an earlier, unreasonable position to give you a false sense of progress. As the stonewalling begins, you think there must be some justification in their change of attitude and that perhaps further concessions will help. This is how the trap is set.

So how do you handle stonewalling tactics? First, remain calm and start testing the durability of the stonewall by asking questions. If they start cooperating again, ignore it and continue as before. But if they persist and you start to feel like offering them concessions, that is a warning sign to try something different.

First, keep the conversation going by continuously asking for something slightly different. Couch your requests in language that makes you appear reasonable and seeking a resolution.

Second, do not let your judgment be clouded by the progress you made earlier in the negotiations. Remember, if your counterparty had adopted this stance at the start of the negotiation, you would have quickly decided that there was no point negotiating and stopped the process. So don't evaluate their past behaviour any differently just because they start stonewalling later.

Third, challenge the tactic head-on. Make their implicit behaviour explicit. Politely call their bluff. "I notice that we were making progress and now you are slowing the process down. What is going on?" Then wait until they are ready to begin negotiating again. Give nothing away unilaterally. If you feel it gets to a point where you have to walk away, carry through with the ultimatum or your negotiation credibility and power will be damaged.

Top Questions to Ask:

- Can you summarise where we have got to so far?
- Can you confirm your expectations of this meeting?
- Can you agree the timelines for this process?
- What do you propose as the agenda for the next meeting?
- Can we discuss and agree on the process and how we run this meeting?
- How much time do you need to discuss this issue?
- Can you let us know when you want to come back and discuss this issue?
- We had a good process initially. Can you explain your change of attitude?
- What are the reasons that are stopping you from contributing to the discussions?
- Before we leave the table, can we summarise where we are so far in the negotiation? (Repeated at the end of every meeting.)

Stonewalling Game

Antidote in Action

Take It:

Keep calm, be assertive and take control.

Explore It:

Use the top questions above.

(Name It:)

Find a non-adversarial way to call the tactics and change the behaviours. Refocus the negotiation on the problem at hand.

"Suddenly we're not making any real progress. I notice that you're refusing to answer any of our questions or discuss any of the issues. Can you let me know the reasons for your sudden change of behaviour?"

Change It:

Propose new dynamics and focus for the negotiation.

"Let's take a time out and come back when you feel able to have a more productive conversation about the issues on the agenda. Tell us how much time you need."

10. Emotional Outburst Game

Your counterparty becomes deliberately angry, upset and distressed and disrupts the negotiation to gain an advantage in the deal.

It is a difficult negotiation for both sides. You're under time constraints and have mounting pressure from your stakeholders. You begin to discuss your own requirements and the atmosphere is tense, but nothing prepares you for the sudden emotional outburst from your counterparty. They appear angry and upset. Their voices are raised and harsh. Their body language is aggressive and hostile. They accuse you of excessive demands, misrepresentation, challenges to their authority and even destroying their reputation in the market. You are faced with a tirade of criticism and condemnation and every attack hits a nerve. They tear up the joint document you've been working on and leave the pieces on the table. The negotiation is in tatters. Your working relationship feels beyond repair.

You feel undermined and demoralised by the wave of emotion radiating from across the table. You also feel anger and instinctively want to strike back. They are attacking your team and it's your job to defend them and your position. And in that moment, you lose control and you begin shouting at your counterparty. The negotiation becomes a farce. You realise you should have taken a break a long time ago, so belatedly you suggest a time out to cool down. Your counterparty is obviously upset about your requirements as these seemed to trigger the outburst.

You know that your reaction was wrong. What concessions can you make to repair the relationship with your counterparty? It's up to you, isn't it, to save the deal? Or have they forced you into this position of feeling guilt, embarrassment and self-reproach by performing the Emotional Outburst Game?

Emotional Outburst Game

NOT a negotiation trick:

When you assess your counterparty's emotional outburst and find a sincere and legitimate reason behind their reaction, then you know that this is not a trick.

Probably a negotiation trick:

When your counterparty's emotional outburst appears to have no foundation and you feel pressured into giving them concessions as a result of their behaviour, then you are looking at some stylish role playing in the Emotional Outburst game.

What to do:

When your counterparty uses the Emotional Outburst game as a negotiation tactic they are deliberately shifting attention away from important issues to push for concessions by using dramatic behaviour. They hope that your natural reaction will become defensive and hit back. By doing so, the negotiation will simply degrade into an argument and one that will be difficult for you to win.

First recognise that this might simply be an artificial and very deliberate response that has been planned in advance by your counterparty. They want you to react badly because that is how they gain an advantage, so don't. Remain silent and let your counterparty assert their views, however hostile or aggressive. It will be uncomfortable, but the first part of the solution is to just sit there and take it.

In the antidotes to all the games in this book, the first stage is always Take It: to take responsibility for your own thinking, feeling and behaviour and this is central to an effective solution. You cannot negotiate effectively in an emotional thunderstorm. Suggest a break, if only to give yourself time to think and let your counterparty calm down.

Listen respectfully and acknowledge any legitimacy in your counterparty's points and feelings, even if you don't agree with them. Acknowledge their anger and if required, offer an apology, even if it is just for the current "bad situation." It is very important to help them save face, and to allow them to give up their anger without further loss of face.

Never give concessions to resolve an emotional outburst. That would be like rewarding a two year old for their tantrum. It would only reward them with a pay off to the game and encourage them into further performances. Have the confidence that you can solve the problem with tactful questions and calm behaviour and then generate creative options for your mutual benefit.

Top Questions to Ask:

- I apologise for any upset we have caused you. Can we take a break so we can consider how to resolve this issue?
- Can you let us know the background to this problem?
- Why have you not raised this issue with us before now?
- How is this damaging your position?
- What are the drivers behind this?
- Which is the top priority for you?
- Can you let us know when you want to come back and discuss this issue?
- We had a good process initially. Can you explain your change of attitude?

- These are sensitive issues so how best do you suggest we approach them?
- Before we leave the table, can we summarise where we are so far in the negotiation? (Repeated at the end of every meeting.)

Emotional Outburst Game

Antidote in Action

Take It:

Keep calm, be assertive and take control.

Explore It:

Use the top questions above.

(Name It:)

Find a non-adversarial way to call the tactics and change the behaviours. Refocus the negotiation on the problem at hand.

"I can see you are extremely angry and frustrated by this but it has been on the table since the start of the negotiation. Can you let me know the reasons for your sudden change of behaviour?"

Change It:

Propose new dynamics and focus for the negotiation.

"This isn't helping us reach an agreement. Let's take a break and discuss how best to approach this issue from a more practical and productive perspective."

11. Scrambled Eggs Game

Your counterparty deliberately makes the deal extremely complicated to confuse you or distract you in order to get a better deal for themselves.

When you started negotiating this particular deal, the issues seemed straightforward. You agreed an agenda and the list of issues that comprised the deal. Your counterparty has been extremely open and in every meeting has provided you with detailed information, analyses, complex charts and diagrams and extensive arguments for each point.

You start to feel overwhelmed with the information they are providing. The language they use is highly technical and you don't feel qualified to join the debate. In fact, you really want someone to translate what is being said into your language. The analysis they provide is exhaustive and far-reaching. You are impressed with their knowledge and expertise. They really do appear to know what they are talking about and have gone to great lengths to help you understand the issues from their side.

Yet you feel you're losing sight of what is important. Is all this information really necessary? Sometimes you feel they say one thing in a meeting and then seem to contradict themselves in another. But you are not sure any more. You wonder if they are using all this information as a delaying tactic, but they are actually pushing to keep to the original deadline. Considering how open and thorough they have been, surely you should put aside your doubts and let them, the experts, guide you through this deal?

When you're confused, distracted by detail and don't feel you're talking the same language, you need to trust your instincts and not the apparently "expert" counterparty. Consider carefully whether all the

Scrambled Eggs Game

information is really necessary or whether your counterparty is trying to gain an advantage by playing the Scrambled Eggs Game.

NOT a negotiation trick:

It is not a negotiation trick when your counterparty provides information which is essential and which provides clarity and greater transparency to the deal issues.

Probably a negotiation trick:

When the counterparty floods you with facts and figures that are not necessarily relevant and cause greater confusion rather than clarity to the deal, they are using the Scrambled Eggs Game to distract and mislead you.

What to do:

Scrambled Eggs is a game of information overload to create deliberate confusion. The biggest challenge is to determine what information is essential to the deal and what is simply there to distract you. Negotiations need to be conducted with a structured approach. The Scrambler wants to create disorder because they know you can make mistakes when you are confused.

You need to be forensic in your questions and ask consistently what is important in the huge amount of information thrown at you. Have the courage to say "I don't understand" and keep asking your questions until you do.

Create order out of the chaos that your counterparty has conjured. Insist that every issue must be discussed one at a time and be strict on this. Don't let them distract you with other issues or move the topic away.

Scrambled Eggs Game

Take control of the subjects rather than following the Scrambler's lead and pay very close attention to what they are saying. Look for inconsistencies in their responses.

The key is to never agree to anything you do not understand, because, if you do, the Scrambler wins.

Top Questions to Ask:

- Can you go through the implications again?
- Is it possible for you to focus on just one issue at a time?
- Can we stick to the agenda we agreed and not go off on tangents?
- Why is this essential?
- What exactly did you mean by that?
- Why is this relevant to the main issue?
- Can you explain why these figures differ from the ones you presented last week?
- How did you make your assumptions?
- Can you give me the reason behind this?
- Before we leave the table, can we summarise where we are so far in the negotiation? (Repeated at the end of every meeting.)

Scrambled Eggs Game

Antidote in Action

Take It:

Keep calm, be assertive and take control.

Explore It:

Use the top questions above.

(Name It:)

Find a non-adversarial way to call the tactics and change the behaviours. Refocus the negotiation on the problem at hand.

"You're giving us a great deal of information which is irrelevant and just clouding the issue. We need a clear and rational debate on the issues so let's stick to the basic facts."

Change It:

Propose new dynamics and focus for the negotiation.

"Let's put aside the analytics which are providing more confusion than clarity and go back to the basics."

12. The Hole in my Pocket Game

They really want the deal, but suddenly they claim the budget has all but gone and they need a huge discount.

The negotiations have been going very well up to this point. You and your counterparty have been able to find good options and have reached strong mutual agreements across a wide range of items in the deal. And as a big bonus, the relationship feels right and the atmosphere between the teams is one of collaboration rather than competition. At last you feel that you really do get this "win-win" stuff. The finishing line is close.

But today is different. Today your counterparty is humble and apologetic. They reiterate how much synergy there is in the deal between you and how much they still want it. But now there is no money. Back at their office the allocated budget has gone. They are sorry, they want to keep everything agreed so far, but you are going to need to offer a massive reduction in price to get to the handshake and dotted line. They hope you understand.

You keep calm and ask them what new number they have in mind and when they tell you, all of your energy goes into keeping a straight face. Do they seriously think you can consider such a massive discount? You still want the deal, (your management need it) but this is suddenly outside your mandate, by some distance. It happens. We all have cash flow issues from time to time and need charity. But there is a big difference between genuine, sudden hardship and a game of Hole in my Pocket.

NOT a negotiation trick:

If, or when there really is no money, or the numbers in their mandate have been changed by their senior management.

Probably a negotiation trick:

When nothing has changed, the money is there, but they claim poverty as a tactic for driving the price down.

What to do:

You may immediately feel that a deal is impossible, being so far outside the mandate, but to walk away without exploring new options is too soon. Keep in mind that you and your management want this deal, and so does your counterparty, or else they would not still be at the table. Creative options and some tenacity are required.

Having established what their new budget numbers are, you can now set about reconstructing the deal. Work backwards asking them which of the elements of the deal they would like to continue with, given their new budget. Keep entertaining the possibility that a new deal can be done, inviting them to choose how they would like to spend the money they have.

How your counterparty reacts to your new, creative approach will be telling. If they immediately engage, cutting items from their wish list and working with you to spend their money to best effect, then it might not be a game. Indeed, if they are genuine, they will be realistic and may well offer to withdraw from the negotiations altogether.

But if they take a position that they still need the whole deal *and* want the huge reduction, then something else is going on. They are going for "win-lose". You can't accept that, nor take it back to your management. You are going to need some fine questions to explore new options and get at what is really going on.

The Hole in my Pocket Game

Top Questions to Ask:

- What happens if you can't get this deal?
- Can you take a "no deal" back to your management?
- Is your management aware that these new numbers are way outside any industry standard pricing model?
- Can I suggest we now use industry standard terms and pricing to get a fair deal?
- If that is your final number, then let us get creative and see if we can find some added value for both of us?
- Would you like a time out to check with your management about the options pricing I proposed?
- I am curious about why your management would change the numbers so dramatically at such a late stage?
- Is your management aware of the risks these new numbers are to the relationship?
- What are the changes in your internal strategy that have caused such a massive shift in your budget?
- Recognising that the deal has to change, what is your proposal for your new, minimum requirements?
- Before we leave the table, can we summarise where we are so far in the negotiation? (Repeated at the end of every meeting.)

The Hole in my Pocket Game

Antidote in Action

Take It:

Keep calm and use your emotional intelligence.

Explore It:

Use the top questions above.

(Name It:)

Find a non-punishing way to surface what is really going on (if you feel that the risk is worth it).

"Your management has put you in a difficult decision. What else is going on that you can share with me that might give us a new way forward?"

Or

"Your management will know we can't close using these numbers, so why are they insisting you negotiate from this weak position?

Change It:

Propose new, creative options for negotiation.

"Can I suggest you take our list of deal items and pricing and ask your management what they would like you to do?"

13. All Change Game

They change the lead negotiator on their team to reset the rules in their favour.

You have been negotiating a complex deal for many months and have built a good relationship with your counterparty, particularly with the lead negotiator. This person listens to you and really wants to understand your issues. You have made huge progress because of this and you have both gained some valuable concessions. The discussions have been open and pleasant and the process is felt to be good on both sides of the table.

You receive an email (not even a call) informing you that the lead negotiator of your counterparty is to be replaced with immediate effect. You assume that the replacement will be one of the existing deal team, as they know the status of the deal so far. No other name is given. You arrive at the next scheduled meeting and find there is a completely new set of people sitting at the negotiation table. They come across as experienced negotiators but none of them have any knowledge of the deal you've been working on. The new lead announces new rules and a "new focus" for the deal.

You feel angry and frustrated. You refer back to the written minutes and a summary of the agreed rules with the previous team. The new lead reiterates that it's "all change" and suggests a different process for going forward.

You feel annoyed. You are not being treated with any respect. All the work you've done has been swept away by the "new broom" and you feel powerless. There could be a legitimate excuse for replacing the deal team or, as they apparently want to revoke any prior agreements, it really does look as if you're facing the damaging and destructive All Change Game.

All Change Game

NOT a negotiation trick:

When the lead negotiator of your counterparty discusses the requirement to change the team in advance and explains the handover process with you. They are also open to agreeing a joint MOU (Memorandum of Understanding) between the two companies of the status of the deal and outstanding issues.

Probably a negotiation trick:

When the new lead negotiator refuses to discuss previous minutes and agreements and insists on implementing new rules, then the All Change Game is being used to change the balance of power to their benefit and impose a worse deal for you.

What to do:

Your initial reaction may be anger, perhaps even despair, so take an immediate time out. Take the time to do the preparation that you would do before the start of any new negotiation. Research the background of the new deal team and find out what you can about the reasons for the change. Consult your senior management and agree a new strategy for going forward. Once you have internal backing, you can go back to the negotiations and discuss the various options you have agreed.

Take the initiative and propose an agenda that includes discussion of new rules and process. Circulate the draft MOU which you have prepared covering the status of the deal so far.

If they suggest that they lack authority to agree to an MOU, suggest they find someone across the table or someone internally that does. They may also refuse to accept the previous team's concessions, saying that

All Change Game

they were outside their mandate. Explain that, in all your previous discussions, all aspects of the deal were subject to management approval and the deal will need to be considered as a whole package.

Therefore, every issue is still on the table for discussion. The MOU simply states where the deal is to date. Suggest your lawyers discuss the MOU separately while you discuss the rules, process and structure of the deal.

Be positive, direct and forthright. You do have real power. They want to do this deal and they have to work with you to get it. Regain control of the process and re-anchor your position.

Top Questions to Ask:

- What are the reasons behind the change of the deal team?
- Can we use this initial meeting to review the status of the deal?
- As you're requesting new rules, can we first discuss and agree how we run these meetings?
- What are your thoughts on the current deal structure?
- What changes do you propose to the current deal process in place?
- What outstanding issues do you wish to add to the agenda?
- As noted in the minutes, we agreed these issues, so can you explain your reasons for wanting to discuss them again?
- You say you're losing out and cannot get management approval. What are your suggestions for an acceptable replacement?
- Can both sides agree on a joint MOU before the next meeting?

All Change Game

- Before we leave the table, can we summarise where we are so far in the negotiation? (Repeated at the end of every meeting)

All Change Game

Antidote in Action

Take It:

Keep calm, be assertive and take control.

Explore It:

Use the top questions above.

(Name It:)

Find a non-adversarial way to call the tactics and retain your power in the room. Re-anchor the deal from your perspective.

"The changes to your team do set us back a few steps, so let's use this initial meeting to discuss and agree a draft MOU between our two companies."

Change It:

Propose new dynamics and focus for the negotiation.

"Let's agree a process for how we reassess any previous agreements looking at the cost benefits for both sides and bringing new suggestions to the table."

14. The Better Offer Game

Suddenly they have a better offer from a new, unknown competitor and they need you to make a significant concession.

You are close to your mandate limits, but you are satisfied that your counterparty is also close to theirs. The negotiation process has been efficient, both sides have traded well and made concessions and both of you remain within that vital zone where a "win-win" agreement can still be reached. You are cautious, but it would seem that the deal is about to close.

And then, seemingly from out of nowhere, they announce that they have a better offer from a competitor of yours. And furthermore, this new competitor is going to greatly undercut the deal, so your counterparty now needs you to make some significant concessions to keep the deal alive.

You will be way outside your mandate. The deal is hanging by a thread and you feel all your energy at the negotiation table is going into keeping calm. You know that it is a competitive world out there. You know that your counterparty needs to shop around for the best deal, and if you were in their position, you would be doing the same. But this is right at the end of the process. You can't accommodate this within your mandate, so somehow you need to test if this is real, or if they are using the tactic of the Better Offer Game.

NOT a negotiation trick:

If or when the better offer is real and they are sharing this as new commercial information that changes their position.

The Better Offer Game

Probably a negotiation trick:

If or when the better offer is completely fabricated as a tactic to get you into making last minute concessions, that under different circumstances, you would not have considered.

What to do:

While a mandate can feel it is restricting your negotiation potential, it is at times like these when it comes to your aid. It stops you from panicking and making concessions you should not.

The new "ball park" numbers they suggest are hugely different and you will be unable to accommodate them within your mandate. But wanting to keep the deal alive, you start to explore this new position that your counterparty is taking. Politely and assertively, you begin to investigate.

But they won't tell you who the new competitor is, they say that they need to protect client confidentiality, perhaps even that they have signed an NDA (Non Disclosure Agreement). They can't share specific numbers at this stage, but insist that you need to move. Apparently legitimate positions, but these are also the natural cover up positions in the Better Offer Game.

But they are still at the negotiation table. Why? If this new offer was so much better for them, why are they still discussing the original deal with you? Why did they not simply email you with this information and politely withdraw from the process, or at least put negotiations on hold for a while? Why waste time presenting you with an offer they know you can't match? Why are they not putting their time and energy into securing this wonderful new deal from elsewhere? Is that not what you would do? Do not reveal that you

The Better Offer Game

are out of mandate, instead signal that a deal might still be possible. Keep calm and keep investigating. They are still here for a reason.

Top Questions to Ask:

- Why did you not share this information ahead of this meeting?
- Why have you come back to us if you have this fantastic new offer?
- Why present us with such vague "ball park" numbers? Neither of us can negotiate with those.
- When can you come back with something more tangible that we can work with?
- What makes you think that our mandate can accommodate these new numbers?
- What happens if we won't move?
- Are you willing to walk away at this late stage and risk that this new offer won't work out?
- What happens if this new deal doesn't happen? Where does that leave you with your senior management?
- We are obviously at deadlock. Can I suggest we reschedule once we have both had time to review our positions in the light of this new information?
- Before we leave the table, can we summarise where we are so far in the negotiation? (Repeated at the end of every meeting.)

The Better Offer Game

Antidote in Action

Take It:

Keep calm and use your emotional intelligence.

Explore It:

Use the top questions above.

(Name It:)

Find a non-punishing way to surface what is really going on (if you feel that the risk is worth it).

"Unless you can share more specific information, we are going to have to view this latest development as unhelpful, perhaps suspicious."

Change It:

Propose new, creative options for negotiation.

"We would prefer not to damage the progress we have made, so let's take a time out so we can both decide how to keep this deal alive."

15. Reluctant Player Game

Your counterparty appears to be hesitant, unenthusiastic and even indifferent about coming anywhere near your offer.

Your counterparty is pleasant and approachable and you feel that you have a good relationship with them. But how long have you been negotiating this deal? It feels like years. You just wish you had something, a tiny spark of interest from them, a positive reply rather than the dismal shaking of heads or long, weary sighs. You are really keen to do the deal.

You keep suggesting options, alternatives, ideas, and proposals and yet all you hear are slightly negative replies – never an explicit "no" but endless variations on a reluctant theme. Depressing, pessimistic responses like; "I really don't know how we could work with that"; "I don't think we can make any kind of progress there"; "This really sounds way too low, I don't know what to suggest". You feel drained of all your energy.

You feel you have tried everything and you're doing all the hard work, which you are. You have even started putting counteroffers on your own offers and you have never done that before. How did that happen? But you feel increasingly frustrated. You feel a strong desire reach across the table to bang their heads together and scream at them to accept just one aspect of the deal. Anything!

When you feel forced to make more and more concessions in order to generate some interest in the deal from your counterparty, be vigilant. They may be putting on their best acting performance, pushing you to be careless so they gain a significant advantage in the negotiation. Under these circumstances, you might be experiencing the Reluctant Player Game.

The Reluctant Player Game

NOT a negotiation trick:

When the counterparty has no real need, financial or otherwise, to do the deal and may have been pressured to come to the table out of a sense of duty. Good questioning will help you determine whether they actually need to negotiate or not. If not, their reluctance is understandable and not a trick.

Probably a negotiation trick:

When your counterparty needs the deal, but deliberately demonstrates low engagement, reluctance and negativity in order to wear you down into giving concessions you normally would not.

What to do:

You should hear the alarm bells ringing when you get a consistently negative response to all your suggestions and no counterproposal. If someone is really interested in a deal, they will want to put forward their own ideas and creative options to create a mutually acceptable deal. When the Reluctant Player makes you do all the work, they are controlling the situation, not you.

So, test them out. Make a proposal, sit back and wait. Let the silence and the awkward moment hang in the room. If you get another reluctant response, keep questioning them about their priorities, but ask them for just the top two so they can't list everything. If they claim your offer is way too low, test them on their calculations. Push them for details and explanations rather than vague, negative replies. Be tenacious with your questioning so you can begin to understand the underlying reasons for their reluctance, if there are any.

If this does not change the negotiation dynamics, leave your latest offer on the table and when they say they don't know what to suggest, call a time out. Explain that you need to see some movement before the negotiation can progress any further. Ask them to call you back when they are ready with their counterproposal.

Demonstrate clearly to them that if they really want the deal, they will have to change their tactics and become actively involved in the process. Let them be the ones to move next and then you can start making real progress.

Top Questions to Ask:

- Can you explain what you want from the deal and why?
- You say this is too low for you. Can you tell us by how much and why?
- Can you explain your calculations so we understand your interests better?
- What are your main arguments for being unhappy with this?
- How do you reach your figures?
- You say this doesn't really work for you. Please explain why?
- What are your suggestions and alternatives to help us resolve this issue?
- You have highlighted many problems. What is top of your list?
- How important is this deal to you?
- Before we leave the table, can we summarise where we are so far in the negotiation? (Repeated at the end of every meeting)

The Reluctant Player Game

Antidote in Action

Take It:

Keep calm and wait for them to respond and engage.

Explore It:

Use the top questions above.

(Name It:)

Find a non-adversarial way to call the tactics and to get them actively involved in the process.

"We notice that we have put many suggestions on the table, none of which you feel work for you, but you haven't made any of your own suggestions. We notice this is your consistent pattern in the negotiation."

Change It:

Propose new dynamics and focus for the negotiation.

"You have our proposal in front of you and you've told us you're unhappy with it. We are going to take a time out and we suggest that you call us back in when you have your counterproposal."

16. No Authority

Late in the negotiation your counterparty claims that their authority is limited and, after discussions with their management, come back with demands for better terms.

You have virtually reached an agreement and are summarising all the issues you have agreed so far when your counterparty, rather apologetically, tells you that they need approval from their management before they can agree to the deal. This comes as a complete surprise to you. This is going to cause unnecessary and costly delays for you and surely they had a mandate to do this deal? Your counterparty assures you that they do have limited authority and will certainly recommend this deal to their senior management. It seems now that they are admitting to having influence, not authority.

You begin to worry. Does this mean that you may not be able to close this deal? Could their management say no, even after all this time? You feel especially frustrated as you have no idea who needs to approve the deal. After a seemingly endless delay, your counterparty returns from their management. The decision is no. They say that their management is unhappy with the deal and they now need to see significant movement from you on a number of issues. Far from closing the deal, you now feel you're back at the start, but now you are negotiating with a third party team of invisible and unknown negotiators.

You don't want to risk losing the deal so you quickly soften your position to help your counterparty "sell" the deal to their management. You realise you're making additional concessions without demanding something in return, but how else do you deal with a faceless management committee higher up the chain?

No Authority

How do you negotiate with people who are not in the room?

You know you're in trouble when the voice inside your head says that you're bidding against yourself. And worse, you are suddenly seeing your counterparty as your ally. Will your concessions be enough to get the deal, or are you caught in the No Authority Game?

NOT a negotiation trick:

Your counterparty really does lack authority and can explain the approval process for their organisation to you.

Probably a negotiation trick:

Your counterparty tells you that their authority is limited when the agreement is actually within their given mandate and they can sign the deal. Then, they are unfairly pushing for concessions using the No Authority Game.

What to do:

Always check with your counterparty at the start of a negotiation to ensure that they have the authority to make the final decision. If not, ask them to bring someone to the table who has the appropriate decision making mandate. This is the best way to keep the No Authority Game from being used on you. If they claim that they do not have full authority, find out as early as possible their actual level of authority. Be tactful, but explore this fully so if later on if they start using a higher level of authority than they declared earlier, you will know they are playing the No Authority Game.

No Authority

The most effective solution is always to do your best to involve the final decision maker. At what stage might they be able to come to the table?

If the final decision maker can't or won't come to the table, continue the negotiations, but with an acute awareness that your counterparty does not have the final authority. Point out to them that you will need them to agree points on a step-by-step basis with the ultimate decision maker. This is far from ideal and slows the process down, but as you begin to use your counterparty as messengers to their own management, they will have to admit that the process is inefficient and think again. Also, their management will not appreciate being constantly referred to.

If they suddenly spring the No Authority Game at the end of the deal, do not give in to their demands. If this happens, you might need to be open to discussing new terms, but only when the right people are around the table. Challenge their claims and push to deal with decision makers only, or suggest that you both escalate the negotiations further up the management chain.

Top Questions to Ask:

- Before we start, can we both confirm that we have the ultimate decision authority for this deal?
- How long do decisions of this nature normally take?
- Who in your organisation participates in these decisions?
- What authority do you have and at what level?
- What are your procedures for making decisions?
- If you don't have authority, who does? Who else?
- What is the process and how long will it take for you to get the authority needed?
- When can the person with authority meet us?
- What do you need from us to help you get approval?

No Authority

- Before we leave the table, can we summarise where we are so far in the negotiation? (Repeated at the end of every meeting.)

No Authority

Antidote in Action:

Take It:

Keep calm, be assertive and take control.

Explore It:

Use the top questions above.

(Name It:)

Find a non-adversarial way to call the tactics and change the behaviours. Refocus the negotiation on the problem at hand.

"We understood you had a mandate for this deal and you haven't signalled that there has been a problem. Why are you now telling us that you have no authority?"

Change It:

Propose new dynamics and focus for the negotiation.

"Can we make sure that the person with authority attends the next meeting before we proceed any further?"

17. Intimidation Game

They threaten you, insult you and use intimidation tactics to get their own way in the negotiation.

It's sad to say that the field of negotiating appears to attract more than its fair share of people who like to intimidate other people. In fact too many business negotiators mistakenly believe that the way to "win" a negotiation is by intimidating the other party. These people are trying to put you on the defensive, so you need to be able to recognise this game and be ready to deal with it effectively.

The Intimidation Game can take many forms. Some people use their physical presence to dominate the negotiation. Others can be rude, nasty and sometimes downright obnoxious. You can face threats that tell you what will happen to you if you don't agree –they think they are in The Godfather movie – or the threat of a lawsuit or other legal action. Other tactics include accepting calls during a negotiation, humming while you talk, interrupting you, ignoring what you say, making you wait for the meeting, bringing in the CEO, President or Chief Legal Counsel without any prior warning, outnumbering you with their people across the table, uncomfortable seating arrangements and even lack of air conditioning. The list goes on.

How do you feel when you're threatened or insulted? Small? Belittled? Under-pressure? Stressed? Angry? Should you just throw in the towel and get the deal done as quickly as possible? Only if you want the intimidators to win. Their whole purpose is to boost their power in the negotiation and make you feel weak. So, you cannot show any weakness when faced with the Intimidation Game.

Intimidation Game

NOT a negotiation trick:

If the counterparty becomes rude and aggressive during the negotiation there may be some underlying issues, or a trigger you provided that is causing their bad behaviour. There may have been a misunderstanding or miscommunication about an issue. So you need to make sure you are actively listening to their point of view and asking questions to clarify their understanding. You may discover that the behaviour change is understandable and not a trick.

Probably a negotiation trick:

When your counterparty makes you feel uncomfortable intentionally at the start of the negotiation and then consistently uses the same strategy, then your counterparty is using the Intimidation Game to get what they want.

What to do:

The intimidator will always try to take control at the start of the negotiation so that they begin in a position of power. You need to find ways to create a more level playing field. As with every bully in the school playground, you need to stand up to this. As humans, when we are threatened we are programmed to either "fight" or "flight". Do not simply reciprocate with intimidation of your own, but neither must you give in. If you feel yourself doing either of these, take a time out. You need to remain calm, assertive and stand your ground.

It is perfectly acceptable to "call" their behaviour and request that the people around the room agree to rules of behaviour at the table. This is to take control of the situation and do something positive about it. Test the validity of any threats by asking them what impact they think that might have on the deal outcome and the on going relationship. Always do what you can to take the focus away from the threats and focus on the merits of the deal.

By being assertive in your response, changing the rules and dynamics in the room and maintaining absolute focus on your negotiation strategy, you can create a more even balance of power at the table.

Top Questions to Ask:

- Can we switch chairs and adjust the seating arrangements before we start?
- We agreed on this during our last meeting. Can I ask what has caused your change of attitude?
- Can we discuss and agree on the process and how we run this meeting?
- Why don't we host the meetings at our offices as it is cooler?"
- Do you need to seek legal counsel now or can we move forward on other issues?
- With so many of your team attending today, can we agree on subgroups to discuss certain issues?
- Can you please clarify each issue that you feel we're ignoring so we can address them immediately?
- You have highlighted many problems just now. What is top of your list?
- We're not getting anywhere in this meeting. Can we take a time out and both sides return with their key priorities?
- Before we leave the table, can we summarise where we are so far in the negotiation? (Repeated at the end of every meeting.)

Intimidation Game

Antidote in Action

Take It:

Keep calm, be assertive and take control.

Explore It:

Use the top questions above.

(Name It:)

Find a non-adversarial way to call the tactics and change the behaviours and dynamics in the room. There is no need to endure bad behaviour in a meeting. Call it for what it is. Refocus the negotiation on the problem at hand.

"I am not comfortable with the language (or behaviour) being used here and it's not making it easy to understand the issues."

Change It:

Propose new dynamics and focus for the negotiation.

"We all seem to have so much to say on this, so let's give everyone time to speak, without interruption, then we can hear everyone's voice around the table."

Or

"Let's take a time out and come back with a more productive way of talking about the issues on the agenda."

18. Russian Front Game

You receive two proposals from your counterparty, one worse than the other, and they want to force you to pick the lesser of two evils.

All in all, you feel confident about today's meeting. Your counterparty will be presenting their next offer and you feel you're pretty close to a deal. You feel that both sides have a clear vision of the end deal. You have been clear on your objectives and believe you have managed the expectations of your counterparty well.

On arrival, your counterparty presents not one, but two proposals side by side. Their reasons for giving you two offers is that they want to show how flexible they are and how they are responding to your interests. They say they have done their best to be as creative as possible. And then they deliver the killer blow. They stress that these two offers are their final offers. You need to accept one or the other. They say that you can decide how long you need to review the proposals, but unless you accept one at the end of the agreed time, both offers will be taken off the table.

They claim they are presenting you with a fair and open process. They say that you can decide on the timeline and they've given you a choice. But both proposals are ghastly. It's as if they've presented you two, different high rate interest loans – the terms vary on each, but both are extortionate. So which do you pick? It is a dilemma. You feel you're stuck between the proverbial "rock and a hard place". When your counterparty tries to force you into choosing a rubbish deal from two bad options, they are probably using the Russian Front Game.

Russian Front Game

NOT a negotiation trick:

When your counterparty provides two possible deal options, but also asks you to get involved so you can both achieve a fair deal, then this is not a game, just options.

Probably a negotiation trick:

When your counterparty will accept no other changes and puts pressure on you to agree to one or the other proposals, then they are using the Russian Front game to steamroller you into making a bad decision.

What to do:

Your counterparty is trying to narrow your options and force you into a bad deal. They are not offering you a free choice they are forcing you into a dilemma. Remember, only one option is a directive, two options is a dilemma, and only three or more options are a genuine choice.

They understand the psychological power of the "alternative close". When human beings are given a choice between two options, it is too easy for the subconscious to stop looking elsewhere. The Russian Front Game aims to make you forget that there are always other options available. If you feel you are stuck with just two paths forward, remember you always have options, even if you don't feel you have them to hand immediately. You need time and tenacity. Take a deep breath, but don't accept either of the proposals.

Firstly, they asked you to propose the deal deadline, so now you have a wonderful opportunity to take control of the deal process. Remind everyone of the end goal for these negotiations, so set out the various objectives and meetings required in order to reach that goal. Give them a clear process path towards a mutual solution.

Explain that you are still investigating all options and encourage them to do the same.

Agree to consider their proposals, but do not agree to either of these two options being the final proposals. Tell them you will use their offers to generate new ways forward and a potential new deal. If they insist on playing Russian Front, remind them that having only two options limits the value and potential in the deal. Begin to signal politely that you know what they are attempting to do. Remind them that as professional negotiators you would both be failing in your duty if you did not look for greater value for both parties.

When your counterparty sees that you're not going to be pushed into making one of two bad decisions, they can either stick to their threat, or continue working with you. Remember, they will not want to go back to their management without a deal having not explored all the options, or exhausted their mandate. The Russian Front is a risky game for both parties, but they only succeed when you stop looking for alternatives.

Top Questions to Ask:

- What are the drivers behind each of these proposals?
- What are the cost differentials between the two?
- Can you explain your approach for each offer?
- Why is there such a difference in these figures?
- Which of these proposals meets your interests best?
- We will of course consider your options. In the meantime, can you review our conditions of acceptance?
- Can you let us know when you want to come back and discuss our conditions of acceptance?
- We had a good process initially. Can you explain your change of attitude?

- Can we agree to discuss the revised deal process at the next meeting?
- Before we leave the table, can we summarise where we are so far in the negotiation? (Repeated at the end of every meeting.)

Antidote in Action

Take It:

Keep calm, be assertive and take control.

Explore It:

Use the top questions above.

(Name It:)

Find a non-adversarial way to call the tactics and change the behaviours. Refocus the negotiation on the problem at hand.

"We appreciate your two offers but are surprised at being given an ultimatum. We will review your offers as part of our agreed deal process and trust that you will do the same with ours in return."

Change It:

Propose new dynamics and focus for the negotiation.

"We will review your two proposals and suggest that in the meantime you review our conditions of acceptance. We can discuss both at our next meeting."

19. Split the Difference Game

Where the counterparty suggests agreeing to a solution that is halfway between the two positions but they have less to lose than you by meeting "in the middle".

You have spent all day in these negotiations and you seem to have reached an impasse. Your last offer that you put on the table was 520,000 and this was a real stretch for you. You already feel you're too close to your margins to make this deal work. The last offer from your counterparty was 500,000 which is way beyond your mandate. You would be giving up far too much value. Perhaps this is as far as the deal will go.

Then your counterparty suggests splitting the difference in the final amounts. It seems like a reasonable and fair approach after a very long day. It's definitely worth considering even though it's beyond your mandate. And they are offering to concede exactly the same amount as you and it must be a struggle for them as well. It's a good suggestion. You agree and propose the obvious meeting point of 510,000. Your counterparty then says they'll need to check this with their management but they appreciate your offer on the table.

When they return, they say sadly their management will only agree to 505,000. So do you walk away? They suggest that, as you are so close to the deal, why not split the difference again. They believe they can convince their management to accept that. And you manage to shake hands on 507,500. Brilliant! Deal done all in one day and worth every penny. Or not?

But, you have conceded a lot more than your counterparty in that final concession. But it's all fair in the end, isn't it? Both sides are happy. Well, your counterparty certainly is. They walked away with a big advantage by using the Split the Difference Game.

NOT a negotiation trick:

When both sides have come from the same starting point, have moved the same amount and have equal underlying value to offer, then splitting the difference may be a fair option to consider.

Probably a negotiation trick:

When your counterparty proposes to split the difference and they have less to lose than you by meeting "in the middle".

What to do

The simple suggestion to "split the difference", is frequently made towards the end of a negotiation and it may at first appear to be fair and equal to both sides. In almost all negotiations, it is neither equitable nor fair. Fairness depends on the standards and principles underlying your offer or concession. Conceding the same amount does not make it fair. Even though it is difficult to refuse such an apparently "reasonable offer", you must resist the temptation.

First, provide information to justify why a simple split is not equitable. Take time to explore other options, other ways to look at the split, re-define what will be split up and what cannot be split up, see if there is a way to find more value before you start dividing up who gets what. Your time and effort in this discussion may reveal options neither party had thought of before and open a route to a much better agreement.

At the end of a lengthy and tiring negotiation, if you give in to the Split the Difference Game, you're taking

Split the Difference Game

the easy, perhaps even lazy way out and you will lose more than your counterparty in the deal. That is why they suggested this as a solution. This game will only succeed if you are tricked into stopping to look for alternatives.

Top Questions to Ask:

- It sounds reasonable but can we investigate the real value behind these numbers?
- What are your reasons for suggesting this split?
- Can we look at other ways to manage this split?
- How do you propose we can create equal value in the split?
- Such a split doesn't help us so can we investigate other options?
- Can we take a time out and both sides consider different ways of managing a split?
- Can we consider all the terms of the deal rather than just one number?
- We're losing too much already so can we consider ways of adding value to the deal for both sides?
- It's far too complicated to just split the difference. Can we review the outstanding issues and look for alternatives there?
- Before we leave the table, can we summarise where we are so far in the negotiation? (Repeated at the end of every meeting.)

Split the Difference Game

Antidote in Action

Take It:

Keep calm, be assertive and take control.

Explore It:

Use the top questions above.

(Name It:)

Find a non-adversarial way to call the tactics and change the behaviours. Refocus the negotiation on the problem at hand.

"We appreciate your suggestion but we can't afford it. We stand to lose a lot more than you if we merely split the difference. How do you propose a more equitable split?"

Change It:

Propose new dynamics and focus for the negotiation.

"Let's both take time looking at other ways to add value to both sides."

The Walk Away Game

20. The Walk Away Game

Your counterparty tells you that the deal on the table is unacceptable and walks out in a temper.

When you enter the room, the atmosphere is already charged. You're there to discuss your recent proposal but the signals from the other side of the table are not good. You make an attempt at some general pleasantries, but the deal team on the other side of the table stand up as one. The lead tells you that they have read through the proposal and find it insulting (yes – they really do use that word), they yell a bit, gather up their belongings and storm out of the door. There is a stunned silence in the room.

Should you have expected this overdramatic response? There definitely hadn't been any signals before today's meeting. No warning shots that things were coming to a head. No mention of any potential deal breakers and they seemed to have been interested until now. This whole situation suddenly feels like a catastrophe and you wonder what you might have done wrong. You have invested so much time in this deal. You don't really have a strong alternative, so your options are limited. You feel strongly that the best thing to do is to call them back immediately and ask them what they want. If you can get them back to the negotiation table, you can help to resolve whatever is upsetting them. You can't sort this without them, can you?

But is it really such a good idea to immediately call them back in? By responding quickly to such a deliberate and antagonistic tactic you might be trading a powerful position for one that is less powerful. Your counterparty might be playing the Walk Away Game.

NOT a negotiation trick:

If your counterparty has been telling you at each meeting that the negotiation is still too difficult for them and they finally and sincerely announce that they are going to walk away from the process.

Probably a negotiation trick:

When your counterparty has given no previous warnings and the sudden walk out is a deliberate ploy to push you into reacting too quickly, or perhaps making a mistake.

What to do:

Playing the Walk Away Game is risky for the perpetrator and gives you more power than perhaps you might feel in that moment. The payoff from the game for them is to have you chase after them offering immediate concessions. So don't. Once out of the room, if you don't call them back, the pressure increases on them, not you. Coming back to the table gets increasingly difficult and damaging for them the longer they leave it. Use this time with your team well.

So, let them go. Do not follow them, call them, text them or email them. Give them some cooling off time and regard this an unusual but abrupt time out. Consider your options and whether you need to do this deal at all. Consider the relationship. If this is a long-term deal, do you really want to work with people as unpredictable as that?

With your team, consider the options your counterparty has left following a walk away and discuss their potential next moves so you will be ready for them.

They have invested the same amount of time in the negotiation as you, so they have shown some level of commitment. They also displayed some interest in the deal before, so that is a lot to walk away from without explanation. They have a mandate from their management and they will have to report back to them so, in the short term, just wait. Inform your senior management about the status of the negotiation. They might request parallel discussions at a higher level.

If your management wants you to continue, wait until the emotional charge is likely to have burned out then contact your counterparty suggesting a follow up meeting. Ask them to propose the agenda. When the next round of negotiations begins, you will need to decide if you are going to help them to save face, or if you want to use their walk away to press an advantage.

Top Questions to Ask (on their return):

- Can you help us understand what made you leave the meeting?
- It's rather disruptive to the deal process so can we agree a procedure to highlight concerns before we take a time out?
- Can we stick to the agreed process of summarising at the end of each meeting before either side leaves?
- What changes would you suggest to how we work together going forwards?
- Can you go through the proposal and let us know your concerns?
- What is the issue that concerns you most?
- Can you prioritise the other issues in the proposal that worried you before?
- Having had a time out, what creative options do you have on these key issues?
- Once we have a common understanding, can you come back with your counterproposal so we can move things forward?

- Before we leave the table, can we summarise where we are so far in the negotiation? (Repeated at the end of every meeting.)

The Walk Away Game

Antidote in Action

Take It:

Keep calm and use your emotional intelligence.

Explore It:

Use the top questions above.

(Name It:)

Find a non-punishing way to surface what is really going on (if you feel that the risk worth it).

"I feel that we have been working well together up to this point. What has caused this sudden change from you?"

Change It:

Propose new, creative options for negotiation.

"I would rather spend some time understanding the problems than walking away. There are other items still to reach agreement on yet, so can you suggest an agenda for the next meeting?"

21. The Withdrawn Offer Game

They withdraw their offer claiming it gave too much away and then under protest, they grudgingly accept the deal. Have you gained the upper hand or have you been cheated?

You have pushed your counterparty for their counteroffer and are feeling confident you can gain agreement. You are pretty close to your mandate and have signalled that. But their counteroffer does not look that good for you. It is beyond the reach of your mandate and you will struggle to accept it. You're already shaking your head and considering what's next.

But you notice that your counterparty looks extremely uncomfortable with their own offer. They explain that they have moved dramatically and stretched as far as they can. After an aside with their financial director, the lead negotiator returns to the table and says that they will have to withdraw the offer. It was made in good faith, but they have stretched too far.

You know it's not a great offer for you and you're outside your mandate, but from their reaction it looks as though you're not going to get a better one. So you accept it. But they apologise again and try to withdraw. You argue that you consider your counterparty to be trustworthy and that they should honour the deal they have put on the table. With what appears to be extreme reluctance, your counterparty reaches over the table to shake your hand and the deal is done.

Celebrations? Indeed, but who got the better deal? Running the numbers, you realise you are going to suffer throughout the contract period. Has your counterparty really been trustworthy and honourable or have they just tricked you with the Withdrawn Offer Game?

The Withdrawn Offer Game

NOT a negotiation trick:

When it really is in the best interests of the counterparty to withdraw their offer and they know that they will suffer badly if they don't. They can give you their reasons and show you their numbers.

Probably a negotiation trick:

When the deal is actually not bad for the counterparty, but they pretend to withdraw it in order to panic you into accepting it.

What to do:

We all hate the feeling of having something in our grasp and then watching it slip away. This is how the psychology of the Withdrawn Offer Game works. You feel you're losing something, so you run after it desperately. You think if you don't grab it now, you'll never see it again. It is this instinctive, knee jerk response that the Withdrawn Offer relies upon, to trick you into the deal.

Notice that you feel a sense of loss. In that moment of panic, you don't consider whether that loss is good or bad. In fact, you fail to consider anything other than something has been taken away from you.

So what to do? Be counter-intuitive and override your feelings. Let them withdraw the offer. Don't chase after it. Instead use what they have shared in the withdrawn offer. Use the information to work out their potential bottom line (if it really is their bottom line), ask questions and test the validity of their position and use this to work out a new, better informed strategy.

If your counterparty really had to withdraw the offer for valid reasons, don't push them to honour the offer.

The Withdrawn Offer Game

It may damage your counterparty financially and it will certainly damage your reputation as a fair negotiator. And if they are playing a game, then you save yourself considerable harm when you let go of a Withdrawn Offer from a disreputable counterparty.

Top Questions to Ask:

- Why do you have to withdraw the offer?
- You say you've moved too far, by how much and where?
- What are the differences between this offer and one that your management will accept?
- Can you explain your dilemma?
- What made you put those numbers on the table in the first place?
- Looking at that offer, can we discuss the outstanding issues that we still have to resolve?
- Can you highlight your problem areas and we can use this as a starting point?
- Can we take a time out and both work through the numbers, as they may not be realistic for either of us?
- What other creative options can you suggest instead of this item that would add value to the deal for both of us?
- Before we leave the table, can we summarise where we are so far in the negotiation? (Repeated at the end of every meeting.)

The Withdrawn Offer Game

Antidote in Action

Take It:

Keep calm and use your emotional intelligence.

Explore It:

Use the top questions above.

(Name It:)

Find a non-punishing way to surface what is really going on (if you feel that the risk is worth it).

"You know your numbers well so it's strange to offer something that you claim hurts you. I am curious about why you might do that?"

Change It:

Propose new, creative options for negotiation.

"Although you've withdrawn your offer, it gives us a good idea of the problem areas. Can we both go away and come back with suggestions for how we handle these?"

Easter Egg.

As we researched this book and reflected on all the Dirty Tricks we had discovered over the years we found we had lots of games to describe. Having written up what we had, we noticed that many were variations on the same theme and so to avoid the book seeming repetitive and to keep it to a handy size, we deleted games that were overlaps or probable duplicates, or at least tricks that did not add enough new thinking.

However, we could only get this final list down to 22 tricks and try as we might, we simply could not delete another. So, here you have it, an extra game for free. Hidden away at the back it is what DVD manufacturers call an Easter Egg.

22. The Nibble Game

They keep pushing for small concessions, which if they demanded all in one go, you would not accommodate.

You got the deal. It is time to celebrate. Around the table everyone is standing, shaking hands and smiling. Now that guards are down, there is laughter and story telling about some of the stranger things that happened on the journey, but bottom line it's a done deal. Someone suggests champagne and glasses are raised to celebrate the next phase of working together. But in the space between the handshakes and the signatures, there is danger.

Your counterparty congratulates you on being a tough but fair negotiator and you feel your self-esteem rising a little as you let the compliment sink in. But in the next breath, they are suddenly reminded of a small item that they should have brought up earlier. They are apologetic and hope you will understand. It is no big deal, just a small concession on your part. That will be okay won't it?

You don't want to spoil the party, so you signal that it will probably be okay but that it can be sorted when the contracts are drawn up. And over the next week while the lawyers agree the final wording, there are more calls and emails from your counterparty. Again, one nibble at a time, they are asking for minor concessions from you. No big deal, but you start to worry. It is all starting to add up. Do you have the most forgetful counterparty, or is this their version of the Nibble Game?

NOT a negotiation trick:

If they are a poorly prepared negotiator and have simply failed to bring these items to the table at the correct time.

The Nibble Game

Probably a negotiation trick:

If or when they are nibbling away because they know you will not move in one go.

What to do:

We have presented the Nibble Game here as happening at the end of a negotiation, a place where it is very common, and powerful. However, a nibble can happen at any stage of the negotiation. And it often sounds like an assumption, not a demand; "and delivery is obviously included, right", or "and that still includes the technical support", or "and that is with the five week payment schedule we discussed earlier, correct?"

It is a tiny item and they express it so casually and, when the negotiations are going well, you don't want to jeopardise the flow and the relationship by appearing mean. The pressure is on you to concede. And perhaps you do, but then they come again, and again.

The most obvious approach is to nibble right back at them. You can insist they make a similar concession over a small item. But this is not efficient negotiating and can result in simply nibbling away all the value in the deal. And as the negotiation descends into blatant game playing, the relationship and likely success will be the first casualties. Smarter negotiation tactics are required.

Nibbles rarely happen in isolation and are usually part of a pattern. Once you notice it, have the courage to bring the tactic into the open. Simply and politely confront them with their own behaviour. Say something like; "I notice that you keep making assumptions about the smaller concessions. I notice the pattern and suggest that this is not helpful."

The Nibble Game

This is a non-punishing way of telling them that you know that this is a game and that you are not going to play any more. Yes, it might risk the relationship by calling them out on their gamey behaviour and you can't control how they will react, but it is a risk worth taking. It is better than being nibbled to death.

Ensure that you have some options ready. Resist the urge to punish them for their bad behaviour and instead help them to save face. Follow up by suggesting that together you summarise all the items in the agreement, both the large and the small. Later on, if they persist in nibbling again, then some powerful questions will be useful.

Top Questions to Ask:

- Why do you keep making assumptions about these smaller items?
- What will it take for you to be satisfied with these smaller items?
- We summarised a while back to get clarity. Why are you bringing this up again?
- We already moved on this earlier to invest in the relationship, why do you need another concession now?
- What happens to the deal if we slice away at what is important to you?
- What other items should we focus on that would be a better use of our time?
- What extra value will you trade for further concessions?
- What will it take for you to appreciate that we are not willing to pursue this again?
- What other creative options can you suggest instead of this item that would add value to the deal for both of us?
- Before we leave the table, can we summarise where we are so far in the negotiation? (Repeated at the end of every meeting.)

The Nibble Game

Antidote in Action

Take It:

Keep calm and use your emotional intelligence.

Explore It:

Use the top questions above.

(Name It:)

Find a non-punishing way to surface what is really going on (if you feel that the risk is worth it).

"I notice that you keep returning again and again for small concessions. I notice the pattern and suggest that this is not helpful."

Change It:

Propose new, creative options for negotiation.

"There are other items still to reach agreement on yet, so where would you suggest we spend our time more effectively?"

About the Author:

Frances Tipper

Frances Tipper is the Managing Director and Founding Partner of SpokenWord Limited, a training company covering all aspects of business persuasion. Frances creates and delivers training programmes in Negotiation, Selling, Presentation, Communication and Personal Impact.

Frances began her career in sales and marketing at Reuters (now Thomson Reuters), the global news and financial information provider, initially in London and later in the US. When Frances moved back to London, she founded SpokenWord Limited in 2002 and began developing the company. Today, she and her team of business experts and entrepreneurs (including Mike!) develop and deliver ground-breaking training programmes in areas such as communication, influence and persuasion, leadership and negotiation skills.

Frances was educated at St Bernard's Convent, Berkshire and Leeds University where she completed at BA (Hons) degree in Russian and International History. She is a relatively good musician, playing the flute, saxophone and piano.

Frances is married with two teenage boys who know, instinctively, every dirty trick in negotiation and use them very successfully on their parents. She also has a very fat cat and two chubby chickens.

About the Author:

Mike Phipps

Mike is a professionally qualified facilitator, consultant and trainer with over 20 years of experience in delivering high quality interventions to both public and private sector organisations.

He is one of Europe's leading experts in influence, negotiation and organisational politics. He helps leaders and managers identify and leverage organisational politics, with a specific focus on developing the ability to influence with integrity, deal effectively with stakeholder management and become skilled at cross-functional communication.

Mike is co-author of *21 Dirty Tricks at Work* (2006) *Political Dilemmas at Work* (2008), and sole author of *21 Dirty Tricks at Work (Again!) (2016)*. He has also been published in various trade magazines including a front cover article for Training Journal.

Mike is a member of ITOL, is CIPD and ITD certified, and holds qualifications in NLP and Organisational Transactional Analysis.

Mike is married with two teenage boys who have taught him more about influence and manipulation than any other learning opportunity. He is also a songwriter for the UK based band The Reform Club.

All of the books Mike has been involved with are available via Amazon.

Other Books in the 21 Dirty Tricks series.

21 Dirty Tricks at Work: Mike Phipps and Colin Gautrey

21 Dirty Tricks at Work provides you with all the information you need to spot negative tactics and self–interested strategies. It shows you how to spot the games frequently being played and how to come out with your credibility intact and your sanity preserved.

So, if you are fed–up of being on the receiving end of constant backbiting and skulduggery from workmates, join hands with the authors and get Machiavelli on the run!

21 Dirty Tricks at Work (Again!): Mike Phipps

Another 21 political games identified, analysed and with practical suggestions for how to deal with these tricky situations. You will have your awareness raised, but more importantly you will benefit from the practical ways forward that are prescribed in this essential little volume for career success.

Made in the USA
Coppell, TX
16 November 2023